HOW TO NOT GET RIPPED OFF

WHEN BUYING *an* ANNUITY

ALESSANDRA DERNIAT

Book Cover Design: Ivan Terzic
(www.nadavisual.com)

Interior Book Design: Ramesh Kumar Pitchai
(www.facebook.com/irameshp)

ISBN-13: 978-1503395046
ISBN-10: 1503395049

First Printing, 2015
Printed in the United States of America

To Austin and Ross, my two fine sons, who are the two best things that ever happened to me in this life. Thanks for making this journey so worthwhile.

Knowledge is power."

— Francis Bacon

Table of Contents

PREFACE

As a financial professional, I sometimes have people approach me and ask me to explain to them a product they own but do not understand. Unfortunately, all too often, this product is an annuity.

I subsequently need to spend a fair amount of time educating these people, showing them what they bought, how it works, what to expect from it, and how to evaluate if it was/is a good fit for them given their unique financial situation.

Here's how one typical encounter went:

Prospective Client: "Sandy, I need help with an annuity I've owned for about 4 years now. I just don't understand the statement they send me quarterly. I don't know what all the different numbers mean. And when I called my financial guy over at [major national brokerage house] and asked him what they mean, all he told me was I was getting 8% on it and to not touch it. But I still don't know what all the different numbers on the statement mean."

When I hear things like that, my blood boils. Nobody, and I mean nobody should own a financial product the workings of which they do not understand. And they should certainly never be dismissed without having all of their questions answered satisfactorily, completely, and thoroughly.

Another example: While reviewing Client "Z"'s insurance products he brings out an annuity he purchased approximately 6 years earlier at the suggestion of his financial adviser. He understands perfectly how the product works but is a little concerned about the annuity's performance. He is expecting to retire the following year (at age 70) and will need to draw upon this annuity for his retirement income. Upon investigation, I find he had cause for concern. He had been sold an annuity without any guaranteed growth and with fees so high they basically wiped out any gain that did occur in his subaccounts. The value of the annuity was a little less than he had started with! (Fortunately, I was able to help him obtain something better, even at that late date.)

In my opinion, anyone who is sold a product s/he does not understand has been ripped off. Anyone who is sold a product that is not suitable for her or him has been ripped off. And anyone summarily dismissed out of hand without having her or his questions answered satisfactorily continues to be ripped off.

But despite the industry's penchant for presenting annuities as complex, mysterious products, the annuity is basically a simple financial product. However, it is made to look extremely complicated by a very competitive marketplace. There are several reasons why annuities are presented as or look complex, none of which are complimentary. Sometimes annuities are presented as complex and hard to understand simply because the person selling them does not understand them.[1] Additionally, sometimes the seller of the annuity presents it as complex and mysterious so the purchaser relies on him/her as an "expert" and does not question the seller's pronouncements regarding the product or the seller's selection of the "right" product. And finally, one of the reasons annuities look complex and unfathomable is because the naming of the different parts of the annuity are not standardized amongst different carriers. All of these reasons can cause one to be "ripped off" when buying an annuity.

So I have written this book so you have the best possible chance of preventing being ripped off when exploring whether or not an annuity makes sense for your retirement savings plan. The process described in this book is not complex, not difficult, and, potentially very rewarding. So have at it!

---

1   Sad but true. While training as an insurance agent (necessary in order to sell fixed annuities) I was repeatedly told I did not need to know much about the products in order to sell them. Seriously. My questions about the products were brushed aside to focus on sales techniques. I believe there are financial professionals out there who know very little about annuities (except for perhaps how to fill out the application) but who are selling them anyway.

INTRODUCTION

WHAT EXACTLY IS AN ANNUITY?

Before getting started it may be helpful to actually define what an annuity is and what it does.

Basically, an annuity is simply a contract between you and an insurance carrier. When purchased for income[2], the contract is for a stated amount of income (payout) in the future (even if that future is just 30 days away) for a stated amount of purchase price right now. Think of it as buying/locking in a future income stream. That is all it is. But then, to differentiate their products from all the others on the market, the variations on this theme begin. But don't give up hope! You can learn how to compare annuities quickly and easily using this book.

---

2   There are other reasons for purchasing annuities which will be discussed later in this book.

WHY WOULD ANYONE BUY AN ANNUITY?

The traditional primary use of an annuity is as a transfer-of-risk product (as befits an insurance product). Purchasers are transferring their risk of an uncertain income stream to an insurance carrier for a known, guaranteed[3] income stream. This transfer-of-risk is made possible by the guarantees in the product. In general, the more guarantees an annuity offers, the better the transfer-of-risk and the stronger the product. Therefore, when looking at an annuity, the focus should be primarily on the guarantees and **the only reason to buy an annuity is for the guarantees it contains**.

However, it is common nowadays for people to purchase annuities (especially the variable type) to primarily take advantage of the tax deferral they confer. If that is the primary reason for purchasing the annuity you may not be as concerned with the income payout in the future and indeed, the future income stream may not even be guaranteed as to amount.[4] That is fine; you can still use this book to make sure you know exactly what you are getting into and to get the best deal for yourself.

---

3   Whenever the word "guaranteed" is used in this book it always refers to the guarantee(s) offered by and backed by the insurance company. All annuity guarantees on **solely** based on the financial strength and claims-paying ability of the issuing insurer.

4   If the income amount is not guaranteed, the formula for figuring the payout or some other benefit will be guaranteed.

In this book I assume the reader is interested more in the traditional use of an annuity for mitigating the risk of an uncertain future income stream.

IS AN ANNUITY RIGHT FOR YOU?

Annuities sales are on the rise, hitting a total of $230.1 billion total in 2013.[5] Perhaps you are considering how one might fit into your retirement savings or income plan, or perhaps you are looking at several different ones but cannot figure out which one would be best.

To be perfectly honest, as a financial services professional I believe it behooves everyone to consider an annuity for at least part of their retirement income plan. There is no harm in checking it out, and if you see it is not for you there is no harm done. On the other hand, if you could benefit from one but neglect to check it out, you could be doing yourself a serious disservice. Checking it out is a reasonable, proactive step to take.

To make it useful, this book was not written from a singularly pro-annuity or anti-annuity perspective. There are plenty of those one-sided diatribes out there and it is not my desire to

---

5   http://www.limra.com/Posts/PR/News_Releases/LIMRA_Secure_Retirement_Institute__Total_Annuity_Sales_Grow_17_Percent_in_Fourth_Quarter.aspx accessed June 5, 2014

add fuel to that fire. This book represents a balanced, neutral approach to assessing annuities.

There are many books on the market about how annuities work and the various component parts of them. There are a zillion more articles on the Internet on the same subject (with varying degrees of accuracy).

This book is a different. While it will give you information on how annuities work and their various component parts, it will, more importantly, show you how to quickly ORGANIZE the most important information so you have the greatest chance to be successful at selecting the right annuity for your needs.

Ultimately, this book is about you learning how to not be ripped off when buying an annuity. And learning this is a lot easier than you might initially think.

HOW TO USE THIS BOOK

Use this book to not only become annuity-literate very quickly but to quickly become adept at assessing any number or type of annuity.

THE SECTIONS

Section A contains Fictional Case Histories that will form the basis for many of the examples in later sections of the book.

Section B will show you the 4 simple steps that will help you focus in on and gather the most important data about the annuity in which you are interested. The section then concludes with "Putting It All Together": the description of a process by which you can easily organize the collected data, and, after prioritizing the features you want in an annuity, compare any number or type of annuity with intelligence, speed, and precision clarity. (And to make this process even easier check out the companion worksheets on my website: www.AlessandraDerniat.com.)

Section C is all about Wrapping It Up. There are discussions about how to buy an annuity safely, why annuities are so controversial, when (and why) to get rid of an annuity sales adviser, a note about fiduciary duty, what a Certified Annuity Specialist is and what to do if you already own an annuity. Finally, there is a critique of our fictional clients and advisers and some closing notes.

WHY THIS BOOK IS IMPORTANT TO YOU

The information in this book is important because it will help you determine whether or not the financial professional with whom you are working (whether it is an life agent, a registered representative, a Certified Financial Planner (CFP®), or the "Vice-President of Investments" at a major brokerage house) actually knows what s/he is talking about and has explained fully the salient points of the particular annuity you are considering. After applying the process in this book you will have clarified what is important to you, know what questions to ask, and will be safeguarding your financial future.

I am convinced if you read, understand, and apply the information in this book you will not only be able to speak knowledgeably on the subject but you will never buy a product you don't understand, or buy a product that is not suitable for you. You will not get ripped off!

Your retirement is important to you. Use the information in this book to make it a great retirement.

SECTION A

FICTIONAL CASE STUDIES

It is easier to outline 3 fictional case histories here and then refer back to them throughout the book as examples rather than make up new examples every time one is needed.

Following are the 3 fictional case studies that will be referred to throughout the book. The case studies depict typical scenarios for 3 different types of investors: those who don't use a financial adviser regularly, those who use one faithfully, and those who are DIY-ers (Do-It-Yourself-er).

JIM AND JANE

Jim and Jane (both age 56) had just returned from Jim's father's funeral the previous week. Jim's father (in his late 70's when he suddenly passed away) had lived a happy and full life but he was not particularly financially astute and did not leave his wife in very good financial condition, without even a life insurance policy to fall back on. Jane was determined this not happen to her. Jim needed to get some serious life insurance in place (not just the measly $25K of coverage through his employer) and she was going to make sure of it. She was mentioning this to several co-workers when one advised Jane to talk to her son, a licensed life agent. The next day the co-worker's son, Josh, called Jane at work and set up an appointment to meet with her and Jim in their home the next evening.

The next evening, Jim and Jane welcomed Josh into their home. They liked him almost immediately. He was a bright, personable, well-dressed, good-looking young man with a very confident air. He showed them various life insurance policies and Jim and Jane selected one they thought would meet their needs and their budget. As they were finishing up the application process, Josh made a casual remark about the economy and the current low interest rate environment. Jim and Jane quickly agreed it was horrible; their savings could not even keep up with inflation with the current low interest rates. With a little more casual conversation Josh found out they were keeping $100K (an inheritance from Jane's mother last year) in a Certificate of Deposit (CD) while they tried to figure out where best to put it.

In a thoughtful manner, Josh said, "Well, would you be interested in learning how to earn 14% on that money for the next 10 years – guaranteed?" Jim and Jane were speechless. Would they be interested? Well of course they'd be interested! But Josh quickly got up to leave. He was already running late for his next appointment, he said, and couldn't tell them more right now. But he made another appointment with them for next week at the same time and promised to get their life insurance application submitted and issued as soon as possible.

The next week Jim and Jane again welcomed Josh into their home. He came with glossy brochures and printouts and showed them the product, which he called a fixed index annuity. He likened it to a pension plan with lifetime income they could not outlive and which would continue on until the surviving spouse's passing.

Josh said, "This product is guaranteed by the insurance carrier. They will credit your account 14% simple interest every year based on your initial purchase price. That's right – if you give them $100K they will credit your account with $14K every year for the next 10 years – guaranteed. After the 10 years is up, your income account will be worth $240K – guaranteed in writing. There is no other carrier that guarantees such a high income base value. And after 10 years you will be able to start drawing an income of $700/month for life even after one of you passes away." He also told them other things about the annuity, all of which were factually correct.

Jane was a bit more skeptical than Jim and she wondered about the safety of their money and how the carrier could afford to make such a guarantee. But Josh assured her the carrier was rated very highly and could make the guarantee because of Jane and Jim's commitment to keep the money in the plan for the full 10 years. Besides which, the state had a program which would kick in if the carrier ever went belly-up. Jim and Jane were thrilled. They couldn't fill out the application or write the check fast enough. Before he left they even gave Josh the names and phone numbers of 4 of their relatives they thought should be in on this good deal too. They certainly slept easy that night.

About 6 months later, around the water cooler at work, Jim was talking to one of his best work buds, Mike. The conversation turned toward retirement. Mike said:, "Yeah, me and Marcy bought one of those annuity things about 6 months ago. With a bonus, our $100K is guaranteed to grow to $215K in 10 years."

Jim thought: "Ha! I got one on him!" He said: "Really? There must have been something in the water. Jane and I bought one also about 6 months ago. Our $100K is guaranteed to grow to $240K in 10 years."

A puzzled look crossed Mike's face. "Huh. That's weird. Maybe we bought different kinds of annuities. Marcy and I bought a fixed index annuity and we've been guaranteed an income of $845 per month for the rest of both of our lives after the 10 years. How about you?"

Now it was Jim's turn to look puzzled (and a little bit pale, too). Not wanting to answer the question, he was grateful when a co-worker interrupted to remind them the staff meeting was about to start. Jim and Mike dropped the subject and went off to join the meeting.

On his evening commute home Jim felt a bit uneasy. How could Mike and Marcy have purchased the same type of annuity with the same amount of money but get a higher payout off of a lower income guarantee? The $145/month difference was $1,740 a year. Over a 10-year period they would receive $17,400 more than Jim and Jane. How could that be? He was confused. Did he and Jane make a mistake? Did they get cheated? Should he tell Jane? Pulling into his driveway, he decided not to say anything to Jane just yet. He would do some investigation on his own first. After all, he didn't want to worry her.

> **Jim and Jane are like many people who do not work with a financial professional on a regular basis. They consult with one when there is a need (notice Jane did not try to buy life insurance herself via the Internet) and readily trust those whom they like and with whom they perceive a connection.**

MURIEL

Muriel is a highly successful research scientist in the biotech industry. At age 50 she is a bit burnt out and determined to retire at 60. Early on, she decided science was her specialty, not money, so she has always used a professional money manager at one of the largest and most well-known brokerage houses. And for the most part she has not been displeased with the performance of her portfolio over the years even though she kept getting switched from adviser to adviser as people came and went through the brokerage house. She is a conservative investor who routinely gives up some gain to obtain safety.

One night she accompanied her boyfriend Ben to a complimentary steak dinner given by a local investment adviser. The speaker gave a presentation on something called a fixed index annuity. Wow! It looked great. There were apparently many benefits to owning this product, especially if one expected a long life. (After all, with her mother at age 92 and still going strong, Muriel herself could easily have 30+ years in her retirement.) Muriel didn't pay close attention to all the details (remember, money was not her specialty) but she was impressed. She was also loyal. Declining to make an appointment with the presenter, she made a mental note to call her investment adviser.

So, bright and early the next day Muriel called up Alex, her investment adviser, to inform him she wanted $500K of her portfolio placed into an annuity.

Alex, a charming and persuasive man, did his best to talk her out of it. "Annuities are not for you, Muriel. You are still a full 10 years away from retirement. Our analysts are predicting a big growth year for stocks right now. You should stay invested there."

But all for naught. Muriel was adamant the money be reallocated. Reluctantly Alex acquiesced. He admitted, "Well, I'll look into it but I don't really know a lot about annuities."

Rather than being put off by his admission of ignorance, Muriel took it as a good sign he was apparently upfront and forthright about his shortcomings.

A few days later Alex called her back. "OK, I've spoken to a few other people here at the brokerage and I've found a great annuity for you. You place your money into a selection of mutual funds; I can help you pick out which funds would be best for you. But regardless of what the market does, the annuity company will guarantee you 8% per year and if after 10 years you have not withdrawn any money they will double your initial purchase price. Then, they will base your income on the higher of the value of the mutual funds or the doubled amount. It's a win-win situation! If the market goes way up you will capture all that growth but if the markets tank between now and then, you still have the guarantee your money will be doubled at the end of the 10 years!"

Alex was happy, Muriel was happy, and the deal was done. Muriel felt so secure and was so happy, in fact, she decided to relax her regular conservative investment strategies and opted for some riskier high-growth stock plays Alex recommended for the rest of her investment portfolio.

Six weeks later, Muriel was at a dinner party where the conversation turned toward retirement planning. "As it happens, I've just purchased an annuity to use for my retirement." she announced.

Her dinner partner was very interested. "Really? What type?"

Muriel was kind of thrown for a loop. "Well, the regular type, I guess. It's an annuity."

"But what type of annuity? Variable? Fixed?" Her dinner partner persisted in his questioning.

"Fixed, I guess," she said slowly. "I have been guaranteed 8% a year growth on my money. That is what it is fixed at." Muriel didn't like speaking about things she knew little about and her face was growing red. Mercifully, right then a man at the other end of the table knocked his wine over and everyone at the table was distracted in cleaning up the mess.

On the way home Muriel felt a bit nauseous and it wasn't from the salmon mousse. What on earth had she bought? What was a fixed annuity and what was a variable annuity and what was the difference between them? And what was this premium thing and why would she want a flexible one? And why hadn't Alex explained all this? What had she done? As much as she liked leaving things she didn't know much about to professionals who presumably did, she really disliked being caught out in complete ignorance. Alex's admission of "not really knowing a lot" now loomed large before her and started to gnaw on her peace of mind. Never one to hide from a problem, she determined to start researching annuities on her own.

What she found surprised her. It appeared Alex sold her a **variable** annuity (not a fixed index annuity), the credited interest rate (often called a roll-up) was 8% **simple** interest (not compound) based on her initial purchase price, and the fees were a whopping 4% per year.

> **Muriel is like many people who use financial advisers regularly and rely on them to manage all or most of their financial assets. These "trusted advisers" may or may not have discretionary authorization to make financial decisions for the client but for the most part, the client relies on the adviser to select the best course of action. After all, they are the experts right? And aren't they being paid for their expertise?**

BILL

Bill is an easy-going, go-with-the-flow type of guy who loves to be physically active outdoors. He owns his own small landscape maintenance service and when not working can be found either golfing, swimming, or cycling. He sometimes still gives surfing a go! At age 66 he's decided to turn his business over to his son and retire.

Bill's income was always modest and over the years, life circumstances sometimes prevented him from contributing to his retirement savings at all. However, he did manage to put away some money and gains from the market built the account up to $165K.

He is fortunate in that his late wife's mother left them a small house very close to the beach. When they moved in about 35 years ago, the property was worth $115K. It is now worth close to $950K. There is no mortgage on the property.

The amount of Social Security retirement benefits Bill is eligible for is not enough for him to live on and still participate in all the activities he enjoys. He knows he's going to have to dip into his $165K IRA.

As a dedicated financial do-it-your-selfer, Bill prided himself on knowing something about finances. He knew all about the important rule of only drawing 4% per year from your retirement savings while keeping it fully invested for maximum growth. He didn't need advice from anyone. As long as he stuck with the 4% rule, he was sure he'd be fine.

Bill called up his discount brokerage house (where he had opened his self-directed IRA oh-so-many years ago) and requested an amount equal to 4% of his IRA. The customer service representative who helped him (he never spoke to the same one twice) noticed he was withdrawing funds from his IRA and offered to transfer him to a financial adviser who could go over his options with him. Perhaps Bill would like to hear about income producing products such as annuities? Or bond funds? Was Bill sure he wanted to keep all of his funds in high-growth vehicles?

Bill was a little alarmed. Annuity? He didn't need no stinkin' annuity! He knew all about annuities. Thirty years ago his Uncle Mel had one. Uncle Mel, who keeled over 3 months into his retirement. The insurance company ended up keeping EVERY last penny Mel had put into the thing. Bill chuckled softly. Did they think he didn't know anything? "Nah, I don't need to speak to any adviser. I'm not an annuity type of guy. I've got this all planned out already. Keep everything just where it is."

The next 7 months were glorious for Bill as he got into his active, fun retirement. But one morning his son approached him with a serious look on his face. "Hey Pops, you don't still have all your money in the stock market do you? It sure is a wild ride these days. Be careful."

Bill shrugged. "It's always been a roller-coaster. You just have to stay with it." He took a look at the paper. There had been some wild swings lately. But wasn't that just normal?

Five months later, as he approached the one-year anniversary of his retirement, Bill was not so cheerful. The market was down a whopping 27% from where it had been the previous year. He felt more than slightly sick as he gazed at the statement. The $115,632 balance looked dismal. But hey, he needed to stay the course, right? The market would bounce back, right? The $4,625 he withdrew from his IRA for the upcoming year was a big drop from the $6,600 he had withdrawn the first year. But he was willing to stick it out. He cut back on some of his activities, canceled his regular ski trip in the winter and generally just sucked it up.

Things brightened a bit over the next year but not much. And just before the second anniversary of his retirement, while the market as a whole was up slightly (1.2%), the growth funds he was in dropped 3% compared to the same time the previous year. Aarrrggghhh! Bill was beside himself. Another drop in income! Not a huge drop, but still....this was definitely not going in the right direction.

Bill's friends commiserated with him over their morning get-to-gether at the local coffee shop. His friend Jeff suggested he check out purchasing an annuity. "Really, Bill, with your limited cash you need to make sure it lasts as long as possible. I started out with less than you: $150K. I bought an immediate annuity and am getting $8,250 per year income off of it for life. And if I die before I've used up all the money, my daughter is guaranteed to get at least the difference between what I've received and what I paid into it. And if I live long enough to receive all of my money back, they'll continue paying me that same income as long as I am alive to receive it."

Bill did the math. He was the same age as Jeff. Had he purchased the same product Jeff had, he would be receiving $9,075 per year without ever worrying about his income going down or going away! With his system he would get less than half of that this year. Hmmm......

The next day Bill sat down at his computer to start researching annuities. Were annuities really different now than in Uncle Mel's day? He quickly found more information than he knew what to do with. A lot of the information was quite negative in nature, with many fancy, impressive-looking websites with many experts (he could tell they were experts because they had initials after their names) adamantly opposed to them. But he did find some positive things. His head was reeling by the time he ended his Internet session.

He decided to take a leap and called his discount brokerage. This time he did ask for the annuity department. The person he spoke to sounded very pleasant and was very helpful although she used a lot of terms Bill didn't understand and went through the information too quickly for Bill's taste. But Bill finally made out he could get a 5.75% payout on the $107,677 left in his IRA in an immediate life annuity. This came to $6,191 a year. He thanked the woman for the information and hung up. But darn! He had forgotten to ask what would happen if he dropped dead three months after starting his income from the annuity. He would have to call back tomorrow.

Bill was undecided. Part of him wanted to just take the $6,191 a year and not have the fear his income would continue to be unstable or decrease. He wanted the financial security. But part of him feared something else: he feared he would lose out when the market started going back up. It always did, right? He just had to wait it out, right? If he bought the annuity now then he could never make that money back. He felt confused and was unsure what he should do.

In the end, Bill's greed won out. He was **certain** the market would be coming back. And he wanted to be there when it did. He told himself when his account was back up to his original $165K (he was that certain a big upswing would be happening) **then** he would buy the annuity and relax. So he cut back yet again on his expenses, stocked extra antacids for when the market roller coaster gave him indigestion and got a prescription for sleeping pills when he couldn't sleep due to anxiety.

Additionally, he jettisoned those underperforming funds he was in and selected better funds – the funds which were top-rated last year. He started skipping his morning bike ride and coffee with his friends so he could check on what the market was doing. Retirement was good, yes?

Bill is a typical financial DIY-er (do-it-yourself-er). With a self-directed IRA or other retirement savings fund and a information from the Internet they feel they can handle all this investment stuff just fine.

SECTION B

THE 4 STEPS TO COMPARING ANNUITIES

STEP 1: IDENTIFY THE CHARACTERISTICS OF THE ANNUITY

CHARACTERISTIC #1

Variable vs Fixed

The **first major distinction** between annuities is that of either VARIABLE or FIXED.

VARIABLE ANNUITY

A variable annuity is basically an INVESTMENT product "wrapped" in the guarantees of an insurance policy. Only those persons who are licensed to sell mutual funds AND life insurance can sell them. An important distinction between a variable annuity and a fixed annuity is that in the variable annuity **the purchaser carries all the**

risk for the increase in the cash value of the product. The cash value is invested in mutual funds. The carrier will never guarantee an increase in the cash value of this product, and in fact the cash value will fluctuate (and may lose value) due to market gyrations.

CASE HISTORY EXAMPLE- MURIEL
Because Alex was a both a licensed securities broker and a licensed life insurance agent he was able to sell Muriel her variable annuity.

FIXED ANNUITY

A fixed annuity is considered a pure INSURANCE product and can be sold by any properly licensed life insurance agent. It is considered an insurance product because **the insurer carries all the risk for the increase in the cash value** of the product. In other words, the increase in the cash value will be via periodic interest payments guaranteed by the insurance carrier (even if the guarantee is a range). The cash value will not lose money due to market gyrations simply because the cash is never invested in the market. (The cash value may decrease due to fees or withdrawals if the fees and withdrawals exceed the guaranteed growth – but more on that later.)

CASE HISTORY NOTE
Because Josh was a licensed insurance agent he was able to sell Jim and Jane their fixed annuity. He could

not have sold them a variable annuity because he was not licensed to sell mutual funds, nor could he have sold Muriel her variable annuity. Either he or Alex could have sold Bill the immediate annuity he was considering.

CHARACTERISTIC #2
Immediate vs Deferred

The **second major distinction** between annuities is that of either IMMEDIATE or DEFERRED. These terms refer to when income from the annuity will start.

IMMEDIATE

An immediate annuity must start income payouts after 30 days (if a monthly payout is requested) or after 1 year (if an annual lump sum is requested).

DEFERRED[6]

A deferred annuity allows payouts only after a specified period of time. After the specified period of time has passed the annuity owner can request income at any time.

---

6   There are deferred annuities with income riders which can be turned on as early as 30 days after purchase so in that regard they are similar to an immediate annuity. The difference is with an immediate annuity income **must** start immediately; with a deferred annuity there is a choice of when to start.

CHARACTERISTIC #3

Single Premium vs Flexible Premium

The **third major distinction** between annuities is that of either SINGLE PREMIUM or FLEXIBLE PREMIUM. These terms refer to how money can be put into the annuity.

SINGLE PREMIUM

The annuity is purchased with one lump sum of money; no other sums of money are accepted.

FLEXIBLE PREMIUM

The annuity is purchased with an initial lump sum of money (usually subject to a minimum); other sums of money (sometimes subject to a minimum) may be added to the annuity on either a regular or irregular schedule.

All annuities are one or the other of these 3 Characteristics.

WHY THIS INFORMATION IS IMPORTANT TO YOU

This information acts as kind of a "road map" for you so you can "locate" exactly what type of annuity you are looking at or for. Do you need all of this info in order to compare annuities? Not really. But you can use this info to rule out annuities that don't meet your needs. For instance, if you know you will be adding money to the annuity as time goes on you know you will need a flexible premium annuity and you can simply disregard those that only accept a single premium. Similarly, if you know you do not want to take income right away, you will be disregarding immediate annuities.

CASE HISTORY EXAMPLE – JIM AND JANE

Jim and Jane bought a Fixed Index Annuity. From our 3 criteria above, we immediately know this is a fixed deferred annuity, which may be either single premium or flexible (this info is not given in the case history). While this gives us a little bit of info about the annuity (the insurance carrier shoulders the risk for the cash-value appreciation, and Jim and Jane have a choice as to when they want to start income), it really doesn't give us enough information to perform any meaningful comparison between it and another annuity.

NOTE: The word Index in the annuity Jim and Jane bought refers simply to the way the interest credited to the cash value of their annuity is going to be calculated. Ignore that word for now; the importance of how the cash value will grow will be discussed in Section C.

CASE HISTORY EXAMPLE- MURIEL

Muriel bought a variable deferred annuity also non-specific for premium. Again, not enough information to really perform any meaningful comparison between it and another annuity.

CASE HISTORY EXAMPLE – BILL

Bill was contemplating (but did not purchase) a fixed, immediate, single-premium annuity. In the annuity industry this is usually called a SPIA (Single-Premium Immediate Annuity – pronounced spee-uh).

STEP 2
IDENTIFY THE CRITICAL COMPARISON POINTS

CRITICAL COMPARISON POINT #1
Guaranteed Income Base

Does the annuity have a **guaranteed** number your income will be based on when you decide to take income?[7]

This number may be identified by various names; I have seen it called Income Account Value, Accumulation Value, GLWB (Guaranteed Life Withdrawal Benefit), Withdrawal Benefit Base, and Income Benefit Base among others. So immediately find out what the issuing carrier of the annuity you are interested in calls it. Whatever they call it, in this book I will refer to it as the Guaranteed Income Base.

The Guaranteed Income Base is one of the most critical pieces of information it is necessary to have in order to knowledgeably compare annuities. It may or may not be the same as the cash value

---

7   For an immediate annuity this will always equal the initial premium paid.

of the contract, it may or may not be the same as the surrender value of the contract, and it may or may not increase on a yearly basis. In the case of a variable annuity, the Guaranteed Income Base may be the higher of the value of the subaccounts[8] or the initial premium or some other guaranteed amount. Since the value of the subaccounts will not be known until income is requested, always use an amount that is known and is guaranteed. If only the value of the subaccounts will be used then use the number 0 here to indicate no Income Base is guaranteed.

In order to successfully compare income annuities you must know the Guaranteed Income Base for the year you expect to start your income stream or for an arbitrary baseline year you have selected for your comparison (such as Year 10). Make the salesperson show you where it shows the number labeled "Guaranteed".

NOTE: For some annuities a special rider[9] must be added to the contract before the carrier will provide a Guaranteed Income Base. Most every carrier has a different name for these riders so find out the name of the rider on the product you are interested in. Most riders added to an annuity will have a fee associated with it.

Even though the Guaranteed Income Base is one of the most critical pieces of information you will use to successfully compare

---

8   A subaccount in a variable annuity is the account holding a mutual fund investment.

9   A rider is simply a contractual "extra" added to a basic insurance product.

annuities, it is by no means the only important number. Unfortunately, many annuities are sold simply based on this number. Investors, weary of uncertain returns, see a guaranteed "doubling of their money" in 10 short years and purchase it with the mistaken belief that they money will indeed "double" (more on this in Section C).

CASE HISTORY EXAMPLE – JIM AND JANE

The "Lifetime Max Income Rider" Jim and Jane opted for when they purchased their annuity gave them a Guaranteed Income Base of $240K at the end of Year 10. Their initial purchase price ($100K premium) will be credited with 14% simple interest (14% of $100K per year or $14K) per year for 10 years. The carrier guarantees that rate and also guarantees after 10 years (if no withdrawals have been made) the Guaranteed Income Base will equal $240K.

CASE HISTORY EXAMPLE- MURIEL

To obtain the Guaranteed Income Base in Muriel's annuity the carrier will credit the initial purchase price of her annuity ($500K) with 8% simple interest (8% of $500K per year or $40K) per year for 10 years. Additionally, if Muriel does not take any withdrawals within that 10 year period, the carrier with give her a "bump up" so her Income Base will equal 200% of her initial purchase price. The carrier guarantees this crediting system and also guarantees after 10 years (if no withdrawals have been made) the Guaranteed Income Base will equal the higher of the value of the subaccounts or $1M.

Muriel's Guaranteed Income Base was also made possible by a rider added to her annuity. This rider has a yearly fee associated with it.

CASE HISTORY EXAMPLE – BILL

The Guaranteed Income Base for the annuity Bill was contemplating is the same as his initial purchase price. This is the case for all immediate annuities.

CRITICAL COMPARISON POINT #2
Guaranteed Percentage Payout

The second most critical comparison point you need to know is the Guaranteed Percentage Payout. This is the percentage of the Guaranteed Income Base the carrier will pay out on an annual basis.

The Guaranteed Percentage Payout will vary from carrier to carrier and will be based on actuarial tables. In other words, it will be based on how long the carrier expects you to live, with a lower payout for lower ages. Some carriers raise the Guaranteed Percentage Payout every year the contract is deferred and some utilize a "band" system in which all the ages in a certain "band" get the same Guaranteed Percentage Payout.

CASE HISTORY EXAMPLE – JIM AND JANE

Jim was concerned because his annuity had a Guaranteed Income Base of $240K while his friend Mike's annuity had a higher payout on a Guaranteed Income Base of $200K. He was puzzled as to how this could happen. What Jim didn't know about of course, was the Guaranteed Percentage Payout. When he finally figured it out, he realized the Guaranteed Percentage Payout on his contract was a mere 3.5%! And the Guaranteed Percentage Payout of Mike's contract was 5.0%! Now, Mike was 3 years older than him and Marcy was a year older than Mike (on a joint annuity contract the Guaranteed Percentage Payout is always based on the younger of the annuitants) and Jim had no way of knowing what the Guaranteed Percentage Payout of someone his age would be on Mike's contract but he was astounded at the difference.

CASE HISTORY EXAMPLE – MURIEL

While doing her research on annuities, Muriel discovered the annuity she purchased had banded Guaranteed Percentage Payouts. And they started quite low. The bands were for 5 year periods and went up ½ of a percentage point with every step up. At age 60 (the age at which she expected to retire) the Guaranteed Percentage Payout was only 3%. At that age, her $500K initial purchase price (which had a Guaranteed Income Base of $1M) would net her a guaranteed $30K annually for life[10].

CASE HISTORY EXAMPLE – BILL
The salesperson Bill spoke to on the phone was quite clear. His Guaranteed Income Base would be equal to his purchase price ($107K) and the Guaranteed Percentage Payout was 5.75% (SPIAs often have the highest Guaranteed Percentage Payouts.)

CRITICAL COMPARISON POINT #3
Guaranteed Payout Amount

This is the amount of income guaranteed to be paid to you on a yearly or monthly basis.

The annual Guaranteed Payout Amount should equal the Guaranteed Income Base (Critical Comparison Point #1) multiplied by the Guaranteed Percentage Payout (Critical Comparison Point #2). If the figure you are given as the Guaranteed Payout Amount is not the same as multiplying Critical Comparison Point #1 by Critical Comparison Point #2, there is bad info somewhere along the line.

---

10 Of course, if the value of her subaccounts was higher than the Guaranteed Income Base then this figure would be higher. But when doing a comparison you need to work with only guaranteed amounts.

It might be argued one need only compare Guaranteed Payout Amounts but I like to have the math "add up" as a system check. Additionally, I like the transparency of actually seeing the component parts of the Guaranteed Payout equation spelled out because it can give you useful information about the carrier. For example, I would prefer to select a carrier which increases the Guaranteed Payout Percentage every year to reflect the higher mortality rate. A carrier who "bands" their Guaranteed Percentage Payout may have a lower Guaranteed Payout for the more advanced ages in the band to the detriment of the annuitant.

CASE HISTORY EXAMPLE – JIM AND JANE

The $8,400 ($700/month) annual Guaranteed Payout Amount Jim and Jane was given equaled his Guaranteed Income Base multiplied by his Guaranteed Payout Percentage. Jim now understood how the Guaranteed Payout Amount was derived.

CASE HISTORY EXAMPLE – MURIEL

At her expected retirement age of 60, Muriel's $500K initial purchase price (which had a Guaranteed Income Base of $1M under certain conditions) would net her a guaranteed $30K annually for life[11]. ($1M x .03)

---

11 Of course, if the value of her subaccounts was higher than the Guaranteed Income Base then this figure would be higher. But when doing a comparison you need to work with only guaranteed amounts.

CASE HISTORY EXAMPLE – BILL

With just the money he has left, Bill could receive $6,152.50 per year ($107K x .0575 = $6,152.50).

Note how the carrier can manipulate the Guaranteed Income Base and Guaranteed Percentage Payout to position their product favorably compared to other annuities. When a consumer sees a high Guaranteed Income Base it naturally sparks an interest in the product. And it is not usually a hard sell when a salesperson focuses on the Guaranteed Income Base and gets his/her client all excited about the fabulous guaranteed "return".[12] Ditch an annuity sales adviser if s/he focuses mainly on the Guaranteed Income Base or crows loudly about the huge return you will be earning[13]. It just isn't so and your adviser is either ignorant or misleading you. Look askance at ads touting a high return rate.

Some carriers may offer an upfront "bonus" to a rider to increase the amount of the Guaranteed Income Base in lieu of a higher roll-up rate. Recognize this for what it is – a marketing ploy. Look at the bottom line, not just the bonus.

---

12 The word return is in quotes because technically the increase in the Guaranteed Income Base is not considered return on investment (ROI). But some salespeople either don't understand this or actively ignore this fact. As a licensed insurance agent I occasionally get unsolicited emails from broker/dealers encouraging me to show my clients how I can "double their money." So the ignorance (or malfeasance) is widespread.

13 More on these tactics in Section C.

CRITICAL COMPARISON POINT #4
Guaranteed Fees

Ah, fees. The bane of all investors' happiness. Fees associated with annuities gets everyone's knickers in a knot. The first thing to remember is there is not a financial product without fees. Sometimes the fees are "hidden" (built into the price or terms of the product) and sometimes they are assessed when the product is purchased or when the product is sold but they are inevitable. So accept and investigate and know what you are getting into.

Fees are important!

Obviously, fees deducted from an investment lower the Return on Investment (ROI) and a lower ROI is not a desirable thing in an investment. (More discussion on the ROI of annuities will be found in Section C.)

The thing to remember, though, is an annuity is not a regular investment. It is an insurance policy. A variable annuity is nothing but a mutual fund investment wrapped in an insurance policy. A fixed annuity is an insurance product, not an investment. And the value of the insurance product is in the **GUARANTEES** it offers- not what it might do, not what it could do, and not what it has done in the past.

So for people wanting to buy an annuity for traditional transfer-of-risk reasons, fees are important to know not for the usual investment reasons but because fees impact the cash value of the policy. And in this case the cash value is important because the cash value usually[14] determines the death benefit[15] payable to your beneficiaries when you pass away.

Fees are deducted from the cash value of an annuity. So high fees means the cash value decreases at a faster rate. If the cash decreases at a faster rate, there is less left for your beneficiaries should you pass away while there is cash value left in the annuity.

Technically, if you don't care about the death benefit of the annuity you don't have to care about the fees. Since you buy an annuity for the GUARANTEES and since the insurance carrier is going to continue to pay you during your lifetime (or spouse's lifetime in the event of a joint annuity) even if the cash value goes to zero the fees don't really matter if you don't care about the death benefit. But, of course, most people do care about the death benefit (to varying degrees). This is why the fees in annuities are important.

For people who are expecting to cash out of their annuity after the surrender charge period (if any) has passed (such as those who purchase variable annuities without a Guaranteed Income Base), the cash value will be of utmost importance and anything

---

14 I say "usually" because it is possible to purchase an enhanced death benefit not based on the cash value. This is discussed further in Step 3 of this section: Fine Tuning Additional Considerations.

15 If indeed a death benefit is offered with the annuity. Always check.

affecting cash value will impact how much cash they get to take home. In these instances the fees are of even more importance than for traditional income-focused annuity purchasers and should be looked at under a microscope.

A variable annuity can have many different kinds of fees. There may be Mortality & Expense fees, Administrative fees, Contract Fees, Rider Fees, Distribution Charges, and mutual fund loads, among others. But **there are no- and low-load variable annuities for sale that are worth checking out.**

Fixed annuities generally have lower fees than variable annuities. A basic fixed annuity will have its fees built into the product (reflected in a lower interest rate, for example) and carry no additional fees. But many times optional extra benefits are available for an extra fee. The buyer must determine whether or not the benefit is worth the extra fee.

Use only fees characterized as guaranteed and make sure they are in writing. Be on the lookout for fees guaranteed only for a minimum amount of time. Make sure you know if there is a cap on how high the fees can go after the minimum amount of time has gone by (the cap should be guaranteed also). Additionally, make sure you know what the fees are based on. Many are based on cash value but some are based on the Guaranteed Income Base (if the annuity has one). Dismiss immediately any salesperson who is anything less than completely transparent regarding fees, who doesn't have a firm grasp on the fee details, or who makes statements like: "Well, yes, the fees can go up after 5 years, but don't worry about that.....it's highly unlikely the carrier will raise the fees." Remember, it is the GUARANTEES that are of prime importance and the focus of your investigation/comparison.

NOTE: Sometimes in the minds of annuity purchasers commissions are lumped in with fees. They should not be. Commissions paid to annuity sales advisers will be discussed in Section C.

CASE HISTORY EXAMPLE – JIM AND JANE

Jim pored through much fine print before he finally stumbled upon the fees in the annuity contract he and Jane purchased. Hmm – looked like the income rider that guaranteed their income base was at 0.9% per year and was guaranteed for the life of the contract. And, the enhanced death benefit they also added cost 0.2% per year for a total of 1.1% per year. Was that good? He looked over the information he had found on Mike and Molly's annuity – the fee for their income rider was 1% but only good for 5 years! It could be reset after 5 years – but there was no guarantee it would stay at 1%. It could go up to 2% per year – double what it was now. Jim was satisfied at least he didn't have that uncertainty to think about.

CASE HISTORY EXAMPLE – MURIEL

Muriel sat quietly, somewhat shell-shocked as she looked at the fees associated with her variable annuity. First there was a Mortality & Expense fee of 1.30% plus an administrative fee of .15% and a distribution charge (whatever that was) of .2%. Luckily there was no contract fee (waived because of the amount of money she invested). But the base contract charges totaled a whopping 1.65% Yikes! And that didn't even count her rider fee of 1.25%. Then there were the subaccount charges of 1.06%. Altogether the fees totaled 3.96%! Her fees, over 10 years, would come to at least $198K (if the value of her account did not drop below her initial purchase price of $500K) and might even be more (if the subaccounts did well). She tried to put things in perspective. After all, she had no spouse or children, and she had already set up and funded a trust for her cats should she pass away before them. Did it matter the cash would be eroded so seriously by fees? She determined to do more investigation.

CASE HISTORY EXAMPLE – BILL

In the annuity Bill looked into there were no extraneous fees. All the fees were built into the 5.75% payout percentage the brokerage quoted him. He was glad a SPIA was so simple.

It is imperative you get a handle on the fees associated with any annuity you are considering. You need not concern yourself with fees built into the product as they will show up as either a lower Guaranteed Income Base or a lower Guaranteed Percentage Payout (or both). But you do need to concern yourself with added fees for any enhanced benefits you may decide you want.

Please note you may not know what all the fees will be before you decide which "extras" (or "enhanced" benefits) you want to add to the annuity. Those are discussed in the next step. So if you don't already have an annuity in mind, read the next step, decide which benefits you cannot live without, and determine what those extra benefits will cost you. You can then plug that info in to compare two or more annuities intelligently.

WHY THIS INFO IS IMPORTANT TO YOU

These 4 Critical Comparison Points are the heart of any annuity. You must know them to accurately and knowledgeably compare 2 or more annuities. With this critical information you can tell in a glance how one annuity stacks up against another and if further investigation into the annuity is warranted. This can save you time and frustration in your search for the best deal.

STEP *3*
FINE TUNE ADDITIONAL CONSIDERATIONS

With a very competitive annuity marketplace, annuity payouts amongst different products are often very close. So how does one make the decision to select one product over another? Often the deciding factor will be one or more of what I call "Additional Considerations". These are additional characteristics of annuities you must consider when selecting an annuity and/or benefits that the carrier uses to "sweeten the pot" as an enticement to purchase their product. Once you have found one or more annuities that are serious contenders you need to proceed with Step 3. This "fine-tuning" may help you decide which annuity is the best deal for you.

ADDITIONAL CONSIDERATION #1
Single or Joint Life

You can select a payout based on either one life (single) or two lives (joint). If a joint life payout is selected, the payout will be based on the younger of the two lives. If either annuitant dies, the other continues to receive the payout for the rest of her/his natural life.

A joint life payout will be lower than a single life payout (based on the same person) because the carrier has the added risk of being on the hook for payouts to two people instead of one.

The joint annuitant does not have to be a spouse. You can name a parent, child, sibling, or any other person with whom you have a relationship and desire to provide income to as the joint annuitant.

CASE HISTORY EXAMPLE – JIM AND JANE
Jim and Jane have a joint life annuity. They are the same age, however, as a female she has a longer life expectancy than Jim so their payout will be based on her life expectancy. Mike and Marcy's annuity is based on Mike's life as he is younger than Marcy.

CASE HISTORY EXAMPLE – MURIEL
Muriel is unmarried and opted for a single life payout.

CASE HISTORY EXAMPLE – BILL
Bill needs maximum income so he would want to choose a single life payout.

ADDITIONAL CONSIDERATION #2
Surrender Charges

The vast majority of deferred annuities have a surrender charge period (also known as a Contingent Deferred Sales Charge[16]). There are no-surrender-charge-period annuities available but they are not the norm. Due to the surrender charge period annuities are not considered to have good liquidity.

A surrender charge is a percentage of the cash value of the contract that will be deducted from the cash value when a redemption of cash value is requested before the surrender charge period has elapsed. Always make sure your annuity sales adviser shows you the surrender charge schedule. After the surrender charge period has elapsed 100% of the cash value of the annuity is available for withdrawal without any surrender charges (if you haven't annuitized[17] the value yet).

Only purchase an annuity with a surrender charge period with which you are comfortable. Most people, if using the annuity for retirement income are used to the idea of not touching their retirement funds for the long term. In general, the longer the surrender charge, the better the guaranteed benefits of the contract. But regardless of benefits, do not purchase an annuity with a longer

16 Commonly abbreviated CDSC.

17 Annuitization is discussed under Additional Consideration #3: "Methods of Distribution".

surrender charge period unless keeping the money in the annuity for the full surrender charge period will not be a hardship for you.

> NOTE: If you own an annuity with a surrender charge period, this does not mean upon receiving the contract you should stick it in the back of the bottom drawer of your filing cabinet until the surrender charge period is over. Like any financial product you own, it needs to be reviewed yearly for performance and comparison to new products on the market. It is entirely possible a different or new product can still work out to be a better deal for you even if the surrender charge period is still in effect.

Some contracts allow a certain percentage of the cash value to be redeemed each year without a surrender charge even if the redemption is during the surrender charge period. Some contracts allow 100% of the cash value to be redeemed under certain circumstances (such as nursing home confinement, diagnosis of a terminal illness, or death) even if the redemption is made during the surrender charge period. Others do not allow any "free" redemptions for any reason during the surrender charge period. Get the facts up front!

> CASE HISTORY EXAMPLE – JIM AND JANE
> Jim and Jane have a 10 year surrender charge period on their annuity. Additionally, they are allowed up to a 10%

withdrawal of the cash value each year with no surrender charge during the surrender charge period.

CASE HISTORY EXAMPLE – MURIEL

Muriel has a 7 year surrender charge period on her variable annuity. However, to keep all of the benefits of her annuity she is not allowed to take any withdrawals at all before year 10. Doing so will not only affect her Guaranteed Income Base it will negate the "step up" provision which guarantees her Guaranteed Income Base will be doubled at year 10.

CASE HISTORY EXAMPLE – BILL

The SPIA Bill was considering does not have a surrender charge period because the premium paid is annuitized immediately and once annuitized, the owner of the contract has no ability to cash the product out.

ADDITIONAL CONSIDERATION #3
Method of Distribution

There are only 2 methods of taking income from an annuity. The two methods are: 1) annuitization; and 2) withdrawal.

Annuitization

This is usually the default method of taking income. Once annuitization begins (i.e., once the income stream starts), the annuity owner loses all control over the cash value of the annuity. The ability to cash out of the annuity is no longer available and the income stream cannot be turned off once it has begun. Additionally, the tax treatment of an annuitized income stream is different than that of an income stream produced by withdrawals. With an annuitized income stream, a certain percentage of the monthly or annual income will be considered return of principle and will be excluded from taxation. The remaining portion of the income stream (considered gain) will be taxed at ordinary rates. Of course, this is assuming the annuity was purchased with non-qualified funds (after-tax monies); 100% of an annuitized income stream from an annuity purchased with qualified funds (pre-tax monies) will be subject to ordinary income tax rates unless the qualified funds are from a Roth IRA in which case 0% of the income stream will be taxed. Always verify with a qualified independent tax professional exactly how your annuity will be taxed.

Withdrawal

In contrast to annuitization, the withdrawal method of taking income from an annuity[18] allows the annuity owner to turn the

---

18 The withdrawal option discussed in this section is not the same as the withdrawal of cash value discussed in the previous section. The withdrawal

income stream on and off as desired and also allows for the possibility of cashing out of the annuity in a lump sum if so desired after income has begun (not possible under annuitization). However, the advantages of withdrawing income rather than annuitizing it usually requires the purchase of a rider for an extra fee.

When an income stream is created via withdrawals from an annuity, the tax code currently considers the income stream from a LIFO (last-in-first-out) perspective. Always check with an independent, qualified tax professional to determine which portion of an annuity withdrawal will be taxable. Do not take the salesperson's estimate, guesstimate, or word for it.

CASE HISTORY EXAMPLE – JIM AND JANE

Jim and Jane's purchase of a Lifetime Income Benefit Rider (for an additional fee) with their fixed index annuity gives them the option to withdraw their income rather than have to annuitize it. This means they can start and stop the income stream at will and can even withdraw the entire cash value after starting the income stream. (Withdrawing the entire cash value, of course, will end the income stream and they will lose any lifetime benefits to which they had been entitled.)

---

option discussed in this section refers to taking lifetime income benefits; the previous section refers to withdrawing all or part of the cash value of the annuity after the surrender charge period has elapsed.

CASE HISTORY EXAMPLE – MURIEL

The rider guaranteeing Muriel's income base also allows her the option of withdrawals instead of annuitization. This rider costs her an additional fee.

CASE HISTORY EXAMPLE – BILL

The SPIA Bill was considering pays out via annuitization. He does not have a choice. Once annuitized, Bill has no ability to cash the product out or to stop the income if he so desires.

ADDITIONAL CONSIDERATION #4
Death Benefit

In general, an annuity is not primarily purchased for legacy reasons. But it is natural people want to leave whatever residual amount is in their annuity at their death to their estate beneficiaries instead of an insurance company.

It is vitally important you find out what the death benefits are for the annuity you are considering. There may be different rules for the death benefit depending on whether or not income has started, and whether or not a surrender charge period is in effect. It is also possible a purchased rider contains a provision for an "enhanced" or "upgraded" death benefit based on the Guaranteed Income Base rather than on the cash value (which is the usual).

SPIAs (immediate annuities) are notorious for having no death benefit (the family of Bill's Uncle Mel found this out); having no death benefit, of course, also accounts for SPIAs having the highest payout value. If you want or need a higher payout value it may make sense for you to purchase a SPIA especially if you have other assets you will be leaving your beneficiaries, if you are in very good health, have a family history of longevity, and/or anticipate using up all of the annuity purchase price and then some.

However, the insurance industry is very sensitive to the competitive marketplace. So there now are SPIAs which do have death benefits (including "refund certain" benefits) so do not automatically dismiss SPIAs without investigating them thoroughly.

CASE HISTORY EXAMPLE – JIM AND JANE

The "Lifetime Max Income Rider" Jim and Jane added to their annuity gives them a death benefit based on the Guaranteed Income Base rather than on the cash value. If they should both pass away (this is a joint annuity) before starting income, their beneficiaries (their 2 daughters) will receive the value of the Guaranteed Income Base at the time of their passing. This amount can be taken in full over 5 years or as a discounted lump sum. After income starts the death benefit is equal to the Guaranteed Income Base when the income was begun less any withdrawals.

CASE HISTORY EXAMPLE – MURIEL

The death benefit on Muriel's annuity is equal to the greatest of either the annuity's cash value, surrender value, or purchase amount less any withdrawals.

CASE HISTORY EXAMPLE – BILL

The SPIA Bill was considering has a 3 different types of death benefit each tied to how income is taken:

- Life Only – Bill receives income payments for the rest of his life. Upon his death his beneficiaries receive nothing – no death benefit. (This is what his Uncle Mel had chosen.)

- Life with Period Certain – Bill selects the number of years he wants guaranteed payments. He then receives income payments for the rest of his life. If Bill dies before the number of years of guaranteed payments has passed the death benefit for his beneficiaries will be the remaining number of payments due. If he dies after the number of guarantee payment years has passed, his beneficiaries receive nothing.

- Life with Refund Certain – Bill receives income payments for the rest of his life. If Bill dies before the total payments made to him equal the premium he paid for the annuity, his beneficiaries will receive the difference between what he paid and what he had already received. If he dies after the total payments made to him equal or exceed the premium he paid for the annuity his beneficiaries receive nothing.

The percentage payout Bill receives may differ based on which death benefit he selects. (He forgot to ask the annuity sales adviser about the death benefit, remember?)

ADDITIONAL CONSIDERATION #5
Cost-Of-Living-Adjustment (COLA)

Most annuities offer the purchaser the option to have the income payments increase on a yearly basis to address the on-going concern of the effects of inflation over time. Payments will start out lower than if a level payment option is selected and will increase annually either by a fixed percentage or some other identified cost-of-living index. The fixed percentage of the increase or the cost-of-living index to be used should be in writing in the annuity contract.

> CASE HISTORY EXAMPLE – JIM AND JANE
> Unfortunately, we will never know if adding a COLA was important to Jim and Jane – Josh never brought the subject up.

CASE HISTORY EXAMPLE – MURIEL

As Muriel was convinced she would certainly have a lengthy retirement, she was most certainly interested in a COLA provision. But Alex had not checked that box when he filled out the paperwork for her and she was not savvy enough to notice the omission. She would have to check to see if she could add it after-the-fact.

CASE HISTORY- BILL

Bill was not interested in a COLA provision – that lowered his initial Guaranteed Payout Amount, right? He knew the value of his house was keeping up with inflation and he knew he'd get regular COLA adjustments to his Social Security payments, so he was fine with just a level payout from an annuity.

ADDITIONAL CONSIDERATION #6
Long-Term Care (LTC) Coverage

Some annuities and/or riders contain provisions in the event the annuitant ends up needing long-term care. Usually this provision allows the annuitant to receive the income stream on an accelerated basis for a certain amount of time or until the cash value is completely depleted (whichever comes first). The accelerated rate is typically 2x the regular rate.

This provision is not intended to or designed to take the place of a good LTC policy. However, if you do not have or have been unable to obtain a LTC policy and are therefore self-insuring, this provision can be helpful.

Sometimes the provision does not require the annuitant to actually be in a nursing facility; it can apply when the annuitant is still at home but unable to perform at least 2 of the 6 routine Activities of Daily Living (ADL). Home care by a paid home care provider must be utilized under this provision. Also, there is usually a waiting period (typically 1-2 years) after the purchase of the annuity before this provision can be used and the annuitant must have been able to perform all of the 6 ADL's during this waiting period.

If long-term care becomes necessary for the annuitant during the surrender charge period, some annuities allow surren-der-charge-free withdrawals. Check on it.

> CASE HISTORY EXAMPLE – JIM AND JANE
> The annuity Jim and Jane purchased had a LTC provision included automatically in the Lifetime Income Rider they purchased. It would be an adjunct to the LTC policies they already had.

CASE HISTORY EXAMPLE – MURIEL

Muriel's annuity did not have any provision in the event she needed long term care. It wasn't an issue for her – she felt she could comfortably self-insure.

CASE HISTORY EXAMPLE – BILL

The annuity Bill was considering did not have any provision for accelerated payments should Bill be confined to a long-term care facility. Bill felt his level of physical fitness was insurance enough.

ADDITIONAL CONSIDERATION #7
Carrier Rating

In this book the word "guaranteed" is bandied about liberally. As an annuity is a legal contract between the annuity owner and the issuing insurance company, **the only guarantees an annuity owner has are the guarantees from the issuing insurance company.** This makes it critically important you feel comfortable the issuing insurance carrier is in sound financial condition.

- Ratings for insurance carriers are provided by A.M. Best, Standard & Poor's, Fitch, Moody's, and Weiss Ratings. Each rating service has its own formula and what is an "A" rating from one service may be an "A-" or "A+" from another so when comparing ratings, always use the same rating company for each carrier. Not all rating services rate all carriers so do your research! There is no substitute for this.

A lower rating = more risk. Only you can decide what level of risk you are willing to take on.

It is important to remember annuities are NOT guaranteed by any government entity of any type. Immediately disengage from any annuity sales adviser who gives the impression they are.

CASE HISTORY EXAMPLE – JIM AND JANE
The annuity Josh sold Jim and Jane was from a carrier with an A.M. Best rating of A.

CASE HISTORY EXAMPLE – MURIEL
The annuity Muriel was sold was from a carrier with an A.M. Best rating of A.

CASE HISTORY EXAMPLE – BILL
The annuity Bill was considering was from a carrier with an A.M. Best rating of A+.

WHY THIS INFO IS IMPORTANT TO YOU

These "additional considerations" are the little "extras" insurance carriers use to make their annuity offering just a little bit more attractive than the ones offered by their competition, thus giving them an edge in the annuity marketplace.

You need to know about them because one or the other may just make the difference between which product you deem the best fit for yourself and thus the product you select. For instance, if the payout amount is fairly close, one of these additional considerations may tip the scales for you in favor of one product over another.

STEP 4
Putting It All Together

Here is an overview of the necessary steps of the annuity comparison process:

STEP 1

Identify the characteristics of the annuity

- Variable vs. Fixed

- Immediate vs. Deferred

- Single Premium vs. Flexible Premium

STEP 2

Identify the 4 Critical Comparison Points

- Guaranteed Income Base

- Guaranteed Payout Percentage

- Guaranteed Payout Amount

- Guaranteed Fees

STEP 3

Fine Tune Additional Considerations

- Single or Joint Life Payout

- Surrender Charge Period

- Method of Distribution

- Death Benefit

- COLA

- LTC Coverage

- Carrier Rating

STEP 4

Putting It All Together

Once you have completed the first 3 steps (the information gathering) you need to put all your information in a format that makes comparison between different annuities clear and easy for you. Whether you do this on your own on the back of an envelope, create your own spreadsheet, or use the companion worksheet from my website: www.AlessandraDerniat.com. It is imperative that this be done.

See **Appendix A** for a detailed description of how to use a spreadsheet, either your own or the one from my website.

SECTION C

WRAPPING IT UP

HOW TO SAFELY BUY AN ANNUITY

This is the section where, in most consumer-oriented books on financial products, you are advised to seek out a "trusted adviser" to help you select just the right product for you. However, this is where I will part company with most consumer-oriented books on financial products.

I am not going to recommend you go it alone. Far from it. But what I want you to do is some serious homework before selecting an annuity sales adviser.

Here are the steps I recommend to safely buy an annuity:

BECOME ANNUITY LITERATE through reading this book. After reading this book it is possible you will know more about annuities than the person pitching you.

START COMPARISON SHOPPING[19]. After reading this book, I believe the #1 thing you can do to prevent yourself from being ripped off when buying an annuity is to comparison shop. It is that simple. Get quotes from different sources. This does NOT mean you ask your current adviser to get you quotes from different carriers. It is way too easy for an adviser to stack the deck and make the annuity s/he wants to sell you look like the best thing since sliced bread. I mean you **ask several different sources for their best quote for the type of annuity you are interested in.**

Get quotes from Certified Annuity Specialists, online services, discount brokerages, insurance agents, or financial advisers. Get quotes from people who will receive a commission for the product and quotes from people who won't. Some carriers will even sell directly to consumers and give you quotes over the phone. Insurance agents and some financial advisers will want to have a face-to-face meeting with you as soon as possible (either in your home or at their office), as they are convinced if you meet them in person, they can "close" you (meaning: they can get you to buy from them). But whether you get quotes emailed to you, over the phone, or from a face-to-face meeting, do not purchase or sign anything, and take no action until you have at least 3 quotes from 3 different sources.

---

19 See Appendix B for notes on how to obtain annuity quotes from different sources.

CULTIVATE SOME OBJECTIVITY when dealing with your current adviser (if you have one), even if that person is your first-born and you love her/him more than your own life. Many advisers are charismatic, charming, and persuasive – that's how they got their job! I had a client, who when advised of the thousands of dollars she was losing in fees from the variable annuity her financial adviser had sold her, actually started defending the adviser. I later found out every time she made a buy suggestion for her portfolio this particular adviser flattered her by telling her he was going to buy the same for his portfolio! Really?!? If her suggestions were so great why was she paying him?

MAINTAIN SOME BALANCE BETWEEN FEAR AND GREED- the two emotions in residence when we deal with our money. We fear losing it (and thus want safe and secure investments) but we also want the maximum return possible (only possible with a high amount of risk). Please! Become familiar with your own limits for risk. Decide how much you are willing to give up (return-wise) for safety. Do not let the twin monsters of fear and greed reign over you.

USE THE PROCESS outlined in Section B, Step 4 and the Appendix with all of the quotes you have found. When you are satisfied you have enough quotes, use the worksheet or your own scribblings to organize the important features of the annuity (as described in this book), rank the features according to your own personal priorities, and determine which one is best suited to what you need and want in an annuity. Once you have identified the best product, recontact and work with the person or organization who provided you with that quote.

This type of comparison shopping is a radical concept not only for the financial services industry but for people like Muriel who are used to using a "trusted"[20] adviser. I mean, isn't that the whole point of having a "trusted" adviser? So you can leave the decision making to them? So you don't have to be bothered? After all, doesn't the adviser have specialized knowledge about these products you don't have? Isn't that what those management fees are for? Well, theoretically, yes, that is what you are paying them for. However, theoretical life is often very different from real life. And the sad fact is some financial advisers are restricted to only a limited number of insurance carriers, or are given financial incentives to "push" a certain carrier's products. Even true "fee-only" CFPs® who are not annuity specialists may rely on a recommendation from an outside "trusted" adviser (who is going to receive a commission from the sale). And after all, I am not saying you have to give up your "trusted" financial adviser. I simply am recommending you comparison shop from different sources. What could be the harm? If your adviser has the best product, s/he should have no objection at all to you

---

20 Sorry, I cannot help but put "trusted" in quotes. If you have seen some of the things I have seen "trusted" advisers do on behalf of the people who trust them, you'd put it in quotes too.

doing this. If s/he is offended or balks at the concept get another financial adviser pronto.

People who do not regularly use or have limited contact with financial advisers (such as Jim and Jane) may also feel uncomfortable doing this. After all, the insurance agent is licensed by the state. Doesn't this mean s/he is the expert? The short and emphatic answer is "no." All it means is s/he is licensed by the state to make sales presentations of specific products to you. And, as Jim found out, better to do some homework before buying an annuity than afterward.

DIY-ers such as Bill may be the most comfortable with this process. But it is important to remember gathering quotes is only the first step in the process – more still needs to be done.

In your quest for quotes, especially if you are looking online, it will not be long before you come across some very negative opinions about annuities. I call this the Annuity Controversy and think it is important enough to summarize what I have found and what might explain this phenomenon:

THE ANNUITY CONTROVERSY

Why annuities are such a controversial subject is a bit of a mystery to me. They are an asset class like stocks, bonds, real estate, life insurance, mutual funds, etc. And for each individual they are either a suitable asset class or an unsuitable asset class, depending upon each person's financial objectives, financial wherewithal, risk profile, age, health, and other factors just like any other asset class. But if you spend any amount of time at all on the Internet searching for information about annuities it will not be long before you suss out there are many financial advisers who are very vocal opponents of them. Here are some of the reasons I think this is so:

THE "RETURN" FACTOR

Many financial advisers are almost exclusively focused on either Internal Rate of Return (IRR).[21] or Return on Investment (ROI)[22]. Their admirable objective is to always obtain the highest possible return for their client (hopefully taking the client's risk tolerance into consideration). Their objection to annuities is they feel other asset classes will provide a higher return. The problem with this perspective though, is that because the end date for the annuity is unknown (in the case of someone receiving lifetime income)

---

21 The Internal Rate of Return (IRR) calculation is commonly used to compare returns of bonds and Certificates of Deposit (CDs). It is the discounted rate at which the present value of the future cash inflows equals the cost of the investment.

22 Return on Investment (ROI) is an extremely popular measure of an investment's performance due to its ease of calculation. It is based on the profit from the investment (amount received above investment) in relation to the investment amount and how long the investment was held. It is usually presented in annualized terms, that is, a certain percentage return per year.

it is difficult to compare it to another income instrument like a bond, which does have a predetermined end date. So usually the annuitant's life expectancy is used in a comparison like this but that may or may not be accurate if the annuitant doesn't have the good manners to die right at her or his expected expiry date.

Another huge problem with focus on IRR/ROI is one simply cannot compare an asset class with no guarantee to one with a guarantee. This is clearly comparing apples to oranges. Because of the guarantees accompanying the annuity, it is in an entirely different category of investment than, say, an investment in a traditional stock mutual fund. How can a product with an income guarantee be compared to a product with NO income guarantee at all? In my opinion annuities are not to be compared to traditional investment vehicles; they should more accurately be thought of as a purchase of a future income stream. This is a different perspective than that of someone who invests in a traditional investment vehicle with the [usual] intent of walking away sometime in the future with their capital and a lump sum of profits from their investment. Many financial professionals make the mistake of applying the metrics of this type of investment mind-set to annuity products.

But most importantly, I have never seen an anti-annuity financial adviser take into account how much return the guarantees are worth to the purchaser of the annuity. While a mutual stock fund may return a higher IRR/ROI than an annuity no one bothers to take the cost of sleepless nights, anxiety over market volatility, and depression over the uncertainty of being able to retire with sufficient funds, which occurs with an investment in a traditional at-risk investment into account when figuring the IRR/ROI. Certainly the guarantees existing in an annuity and the peace of mind along with its purchase are worth giving up some amount of IRR/ROI on the part of the annuity purchaser. What is that amount? What is that worth to the purchaser? Shouldn't that amount be added to the IRR/ROI of the product?

And finally, financial professionals sometimes forget "expected" returns are nothing but someone's best educated (or not-so-educated) guess. Or they are something cooked up from an "average"[23] of the past performance of the asset class. Clearly, past performance is not indicative of future performance and it is well known returns are not correlated year-to-year. So I am suspect of financial professionals who dismiss annuities based on a comparison to some hypothetical expected or average return.

CASH VALUE

The overarching focus on IRR or ROI as described above keeps some financial professionals focused on the cash value of the

---

23 Depending on "averages" when dealing with negative numbers is highly inaccurate. For example: a $1000 investment goes up 100% to $2000. The next year the investment falls 50% back to $1000. The 2 year return is 0% ($1000 start - $1000 finish) yet arithmetically averaging the returns indicates the investment should be up 25%! [((100-50)/2)] = +25%. So why should you be concerned? Because many financial professionals tout the "average" return for the stock market, which contains negative numbers.

annuity to the detriment of the guarantees. When an annuity is used traditionally as an income producing vehicle it is important to know how the cash is going to accumulate. But the only reason to buy an annuity is for the guarantees it offers. In that sense, how the cash is going to accumulate is secondary to the guarantees. When looking at these types of annuities it would be better to focus on the guarantees. However, in the case of an annuity purchased solely for tax deferral of gains, the cash value is of primary importance and there may not even be any guarantees for gain in the contract. In that case, a better focus might be an in-depth analysis of the tax advantages[24] in relation to the fees charged for the annuity.

BAD PRESS

Media reports of abuses by less-than-ethical sales advisers who either lie outright about the features of the product or who disregard suitability requirements and pressure retirees/seniors to purchase annuities with less than favorable features (but perhaps extremely favorable commissions) thus placing the purchaser in difficult financial situations later when s/he cannot obtain her/his money without a substantial penalty or when the value of the annuity has vastly underperformed the promises of the salesper-

---

24 Don't forget gains from an annuity are taxed at regular rates, not at capital gains rates. Always talk to an independent tax professional before purchasing a variable annuity for the purpose of tax deferral on mutual fund gains. Do not rely on the marketing materials from your adviser's office to convince you.

son occasionally surface and are widely reported on. While sales abuses do exist (as in every industry) and while it is a good idea for people to be on their guard, the press sometimes goes overboard and paints all advisers with the broad brushstroke of negligence. The press coverage can give the impression all annuities are bad or all sales advisers are out to get you. This is a great disservice to both advisers and potential annuity purchasers alike. But let's face it, a story about someone getting ripped off is more likely to catch the public's attention than a GAO report advising retirees to buy annuities for their retirement income plans.[25]

LESS MONEY FOR THEM

Then there are financial advisers who talk annuities down because all funds placed into an annuity are therefore not available to them to invest or manage (for a fee). The most egregious example I personally witnessed in this regard was a presentation done by a CFP® who was ostensibly conducting a retirement seminar but who proceeded to give out more misinformation and outright lies about annuities than I have ever heard in one place (or in such a short amount of time) before. His virulent attack on annuities (whether through sheer ignorance or through intentional manipulation) caused me to investigate him and his firm more thoroughly. I found out he was promoting an asset

---

25 U.S. Government Accountability Office, 2011 June, *Retirement Income: Ensuring income throughout retirement requires difficult choices.* Publication No. GAO-11-400, Retrieved from www.gao.gov/new.items/d11400.pdf on June 18, 2014.

management program that balanced client stock portfolios monthly, with a monthly fee for every balancing. Sad but true.

COMMISSION HYSTERIA

And finally, there are those advisers who talk annuities down because the person who sells the annuity may[26] receive a commission for the sale. Ironically, this criticism may come from advisers who charge a 1% or higher management fee per year, which comes directly out of the client's investment capital (thus reducing the amount of the client's capital). With an annuity, the commission paid to the salesperson is usually only a one-time deal and is paid out of the insurance carrier's general fund, never from the annuity buyer's premium (thus **not** reducing the amount the buyer's capital). So what's the beef here?

Another form of commission hysteria is the belief if an adviser receives a commission on a product s/he cannot possibly be unbiased in her/his recommendation and will either recommend an unneeded product or simply the product paying the highest commission. This attitude usually comes from fee-only[27] advisers or planners who wish to have the sanctity of their recommendations unquestioned. Sorry. Being the skeptic I am, everyone's

---

26 No-load annuities do not pay commissions. They can be purchased either from advisers who charge a fee for investment advice or directly from the carrier.

27 Make sure you know the difference between fee-only and fee-based.

recommendations come under scrutiny. Being fee-only does not give you a free pass. But nice try.

Regardless of which particular flavor of commission hysteria the anti-annuity adviser is infected with, **the absolute best way to protect yourself from someone you suspect is pushing a product just for the commission is to use the information and process outlined in this book.** Use this process with people who will receive a commission and use it with people who won't. The results may surprise you.

WHEN TO DITCH AN ANNUITY SALES ADVISER

Now you are armed with information which will allow you to navigate through the morass of conflicting opinions out there, you should turn your attention to some specific reasons warning bells should go off in your head when dealing with a potential annuity sales adviser. Deal with them if you must but if you recognize your adviser doing any of the following, proceed with extreme caution. And don't forget: you've been warned!

- Cold calls you (defined as: you don't know them, they don't know you, and you were not expecting the call).

- Semi-cold calls you. You don't know them, they don't know you, but they were referred to you by the company (or government agency) from which you are shortly expecting to retire. Many companies provide financial planning services for retiring employees as an outgoing benefit. This is usually done by contracting with a third-party financial planning firm. But just because this firm has contracted with your employer does not mean you have to use them and it does not mean the adviser has the best recommendations. Make sure you subject any recommendations for annuities by these advisers to the same process outline in this book.

- Pressures you to have a face-to-face meeting as soon as possible (like this afternoon!).

- Insists on meeting you in your home without regard for whether that is comfortable for you or not or does not at least offer you the option of an office meeting. This may mean they are working out of their car. They may offer to meet you at a coffee shop. But do you want to speak about sensitive and private financial matters amidst the public hustle and bustle of a coffee shop?

- Appears to be an extremist (either loathes annuities with the ferocity of a lion or who believes everyone on the face of the earth should have one). Any adviser who would summarily dismiss an entire asset class out of hand is suspect, so is any adviser who believes a certain asset class is a must for everyone.

- Can't answer your questions about the annuity or doesn't seem to know how it works. This does not mean you should expect the adviser to be carrying around every minute detail of every type of annuity in her/his head. But if the adviser is recommending a particular annuity s/he should know it inside and out.

- Does not thoroughly explain **to your complete understanding** why her/his recommendation is a good one.

- Tries to make you feel bad or seems offended when you indicate you are going to shop around with different sources. May even indicate they won't work with you in the future if you persist in this stupid comparison shopping thing. Good. Let them go.

- Tries to get you to proceed with the purchase because there is "nothing to think about today" and the time to "think about it" is during the "free-look" period.

- Tries to rush you into proceeding with the purchase because "rates are about to change" and s/he wants you to "lock in" this great deal. You may want to confirm with the carrier that a rate change is imminent but you should never skimp on the due diligence process outlined in this book.

- You are told you have to apply for the annuity to see if you qualify[28] for it.

- Suggests in any way the annuity is somehow guaranteed by any government entity (state or federal).

- Encourages you to fudge numbers on the suitability form or on any form, for that matter. Or makes up numbers for you.

- Uses scare tactics to try to get you to purchase. This may take the form of predicting an imminent market collapse and the loss of all of your retirement savings or some other disaster. Being reminded you may outlive your money (especially if you have very limited funds to begin with) doesn't count, however. That is a distinct possibility.

- Presents products which sound too good to be true. (14% interest!)

- Tells you the annuity will save or shelter your assets so you can qualify for government aid if you need to enter a long-term care facility. If this is your motivation for purchasing an annuity please contact an independent elder law attorney first. The rules for these things change

---

28 Even though it is an insurance product there are no health or medical requirements to buy an annuity UNLESS you are in poor health and are trying to get an annuity with an accelerated (higher-than-normal) payout percentage. However, you will have to qualify financially. This is done via a "suitability" form, which does not require any payment to submit.

frequently and you should not take the word of a sales adviser on such an important matter.

- Talks about "doubling your money" when it is only the Guaranteed Income Base that doubles.

- Is not completely transparent, up-front, or knowledgeable about fees. Predicts non-guaranteed fees are either unlikely to or won't be changed by the carrier. Predictions are for psychics. Is your sales adviser a psychic? If so, get next week's winning lottery numbers from her/him right away!

- Suggests you take out a reverse mortgage on your residence (or any loan) to fund an annuity.

- Encourages you to place all of your liquid assets into the annuity.

- Indicates the percentage roll-up on a lifetime income rider is your ROI or your "earnings".

- Promises returns far in excess of those currently offered by the market. (14% interest!)

- Likens an annuity to a pension plan.

- Assures you nobody has better products than the ones s/he are offering. This may be true but you'll be the one to determine that by following the process outlined in Section B.

- Tells you comparison shopping is not necessary because s/he works with (or can quote from) 50+ (or whatever number) different insurance carriers. Or tells you comparison shopping is not necessary for any reason. If the sales adviser is so confident s/he has the best products let her/him show it with the best quote.

- Invites you to a "seminar," "workshop," or "educational/ informational meeting," which may include a free dinner or lunch (à la Muriel in the Case History examples). The topic is usually related to retirement (e.g., Social Security) or some aspect of investing. You should automatically mentally categorize all of these events as "sales pitches." Go if you are desperate for the free meal, but understand the information you receive will be limited and of the "teaser" variety in which you will get just enough information to convince you of the need for the presenter/ adviser's follow-up help. Unfortunately, even those "adult ed" non-credit classes/events held at local community colleges are not excluded from this warning (see "Less Money for Them" above). Just because the class is held at a local community college does not mean the presenter is an unbiased educator endorsed by the community college although it is likely the attendees will believe this is the case (and the presenter will do little to disabuse them of their belief).

- Mentions the word "hybrid" in relation to an annuity. Describes the annuity as a "hybrid" annuity. There is no such thing. This is sales jive designed to make you think the annuity is somehow new, superior, special, or different from other variable or fixed annuities on the market. This is not true. I can assure you the annuity you are looking at is either a fixed or a variable annuity, and calling it something different does not make it different or special.

- Tells you the annuity is a way you can participate in market gains without any loss if the market declines. This is the classic line used to push fixed index annuities. It is wrong. In a fixed index annuity the owner's premium is never invested in the market so technically there is never any participation in market gains. Also, the focus of this "sales pitch" is how the cash value accumulates – which is guaranteed to be a range so it cannot be predicted (you have to use 0 as a guaranteed amount). And finally, most of these products are sold with a lifetime income rider so how the cash accumulates is secondary to the guarantees of the rider. If anyone tries this line on you proceed with extreme caution.

- Presents you with a book with their name on it as the author (with maybe a co-author). This is usually a stapled paperback booklet with large print, many graphics, and speaks in glowing terms about the subject, most likely a fixed index annuity. There is a lot of emphasis on how the annuity would have performed compared to a stock market index. This book is intended to give you the impression the sales adviser is an bonafide authority on the subject and you are lucky s/he took time out of her/his busy schedule to grace your humble abode. What you may not know is these books can be ordered by the sales adviser with her/his name imprinted on them; the sales adviser may have had nothing to do with the writing of it at all. Lately, though, my understanding is the more advanced marketing organizations will help their sales associates "re-write" portions of the book in their own words (with perhaps a new cover graphic) so the book appears more authentic and unique to the sales associate. A quick check on Amazon.com (where the book will NOT show up under the author's name) will tip you off it's simply a marketing ploy. If you need paper with which to start your BBQ, put that marketing book to good use.

- Focuses on non-guaranteed (hypothetical) elements of the contract. The non-guaranteed elements of the annuity contract should be described to you thoroughly and accurately. But the adviser who wants to talk more about what the contract might do, may do, or is likely to do than the guaranteed elements is suspect.

- Focuses on what the contract "would have done" if you had just purchased it 2, 5, 10, or "x" number of years ago. Keeps your attention on "what you would have now" in the above scenario. This, of course, is designed to give you the impression that what happened in the past is going to happen in the future. But as everyone knows, *past performance is not indicative of future performance.* If the annuity sales adviser you are getting a quote from keeps forgetting this, just keep reminding her/him. Better yet, get a quote from someone else.

- Tries to talk you into purchasing an annuity because of the upfront "bonus" the carrier is offering. Or worse yet, tries to portray an upfront bonus as an "immediate return of "x" percent". I've seen bonuses offered as high as 10% of the initial premium. That "bonus" is nothing but a manipulation of the Guaranteed Income Base. In other words, it is a marketing ploy, designed to give you the impression you are receiving something other carriers will not give you. Reread Section B, Step 2, Critical Comparison Point #1: Guaranteed Income Base. Use the process!

A NOTE ABOUT FIDUCIARY DUTY

Fiduciary duty is defined as "an obligation to act in the best interests of another party." Registered Investment Advisors and CFPs® who provide financial planning services are considered to have a fiduciary duty to their clients and are held to this higher standard of responsibility. You should be aware life insurance agents do not have a fiduciary duty to their clients. Does this mean you should not use a life insurance agent to get a quote? No – they often have access to some fabulous annuity products others cannot or will not quote. Just be aware of this fact and use the process outlined in this book to protect yourself.

WHAT IS A CERTIFIED ANNUITY SPECIALIST®?

While you can get annuity quotes from many different sources, you may want to check to see if there is a Certified Annuity Specialist® in your area. Many life insurance agents sell annuities only as a sideline and many financial advisers at major brokerage houses will need to walk (or call) over to the brokerage's annuity department to get information. A Certified Annuity Specialist® is professional designation for someone who has devoted many hours of extra study and testing on annuity products, principles, and strategies and who continues to update their knowledge base with an extra 30 hours of continuing education every 2 years (above and beyond what is required by the state for licensure).

FINRA INFORMATION:

http://tinyurl.com/mpuzdcz

CERTIFIED ANNUITY SPECIALIST® NATIONWIDE LISTINGS

http://tinyurl.com/kaen3yj

WHAT IF YOU ALREADY OWN AN ANNUITY BUT DID NOT COMPARISON SHOP?

Don't panic. Information will be your best friend. Regardless of the type of annuity you own, there is never any harm in having it reviewed for current performance, suitability, and options. Start out by entering the pertinent information (as if it were a quote) in the process outlined in Section B under Putting It All Together. Collect other quotes and enter to compare. If the surrender charge period for your current annuity is still in effect, consult with the adviser who gave you your top quote (assuming it is better than your current annuity) to see if it may be advantageous to switch over despite the surrender charge which may be imposed. You might be pleasantly surprised. Do not simply switch over to a new annuity without checking with an adviser as annuity exchanges can be complicated.

A CRITIQUE OF OUR FICTIONAL ADVISERS AND CLIENTS

So how did our fictional advisers and clients make out? What mistakes did they make? The shorter answer would come from asking "what did they do right?" which was practically nothing. Nobody comparison shopped. Nobody educated themselves (in general or specifically) until long after the sale.

Jim and Jane:
Didn't comparison shop.

Didn't educate themselves on annuities in general or in specific (until long after the sale).

Accepted Josh as an expert because he was a licensed insurance agent (and because they liked him).

Let greed take over – never questioned a return of 14% when CD's are returning 1%.

Josh:

Offered an unrealistic "return" rate.

Presented the roll-up rate on an income rider as "earnings".

Focused on and presented only one product.

Basically told Jim and Jane the state was guaranteeing the annuity.

Muriel

Didn't comparison shop.

Didn't understand what she wanted or what she bought.

Didn't verify the product she bought was the type of product she thought she was getting.

Alex

Didn't have knowledge of the product his client was interested in.

Placed her in a variable annuity without telling her about the fees.

Didn't clarify the 8% income rider roll-up was simple interest, not compound.

Didn't make sure Muriel understood what she was buying.

Bill

Poor Bill. He made so many mistakes I am not sure where to start. Probably his biggest mistake was a closed mind. Because of his family's bad experience with an annuity many years ago, he felt he already knew all about annuities. Missing out on the way annuity products have changed over the years caused him to miss out on a good opportunity to guarantee himself a stable, secure, lifetime income. Also, his insistence on "going it alone" with outdated info did not help. Made the common investor mistake of "chasing" returns by buying the top performers of the previous year (the ones least likely to be in the No. 1 spot next year). Finally, greed reared its ugly head with his decision to continue to risk all of his liquid cash savings while at the same time relying on them for income for basic needs. A risky proposition, indeed.

CLOSING COMMENTS

Because of the guarantees they offer, income annuities are a unique financial asset and they may make an excellent choice for the conservative portion of a balanced risk portfolio. If a life insurance policy can be considered protection against the financial implications of dying prematurely, the income annuity can be considered protection against the financial implications of living too long. There are no other investment products in the marketplace that will continue to pay the purchaser an income when the purchaser's account value is $0. The benefit of this type of guarantee (a person cannot outlive his/her money) cannot be overstated, especially in this era of medical advances and unprecedented longevity.

In my opinion, if you have less than $500K cash assets going into retirement, you absolutely need to investigate annuities as a way to produce income for your retirement. And the less cash you have, the more important it becomes.

It may turn out an annuity is not for you, but you will have the satisfaction of knowing for sure. If it turns out an annuity is a good choice for you, if you follow the process in this book you will have the satisfaction of knowing you have the best one for you. Your chances of having been ripped off will be very very low.

APPENDIX A

NOTES FOR USING THE SPREADSHEET FROM THE WEBSITE

The first 8 pieces of information are simply for identification purposes. After the product name, make sure you note if you expect to be purchasing a rider with the product.

The next 3 pieces of information correlate to Section B, Step 1: Annuity Characteristics.

Enter initial Purchase Price.

If an annuity with a Flexible Premium is being considered and additional amounts of money will be added to the annuity, note the annual amount of the additional purchases on the line after the initial Purchase Price. You must be consistent with the information you are collecting.

Note the Year the comparison figures are coming from. For the comparison to be valid, you must take information from the same year for all annuities being considered. Anything else would be comparing apples to orangutans.

Enter the Guaranteed Income Base and the Guaranteed Percentage Payout. These are discussed in Section B, Step 2: Critical Comparison Points. The worksheet will calculate the Guaranteed Annual Payout and a Guaranteed Monthly Payout. These amounts should be the same as the quote you received.

Enter the Guaranteed Fees (in terms of %) and the Guaranteed Fees (in terms of $ amount). These are discussed in Section B, Step 2: Critical Comparison Points. Some annuities will have only 1 type of Fee and some will have both types. IMPORTANT: Make sure the fees you enter are guaranteed for the entire amount of the comparison period. If the fees are only guaranteed for 5 years for example, and you want to compare a 10-year result, average what is guaranteed.

CASE HISTORY EXAMPLE – JIM AND JANE

When Jim was looking at the annuity Mike and Marcy bought, he found out the annuity they had purchased had a 1% annual fee that was only guaranteed for 5 years. After 5 years it might be raised as high as 2% but it was guaranteed to never exceed 2%. If the fees are 1% for the first 5 years and 2% for the second 5 years, the average works out to be 1.5% over the entire 10 years. Enter 1.5 for the Guaranteed Fee (%) in this case. In these types of instances you always need to work with worst-case scenario.

Also enter the following:
- Whether the quote is for a Single Life or Joint Life.
- Surrender Charge Period (in terms of years). Note: This could be different for different annuities.
- Distribution: "A" if you plan on annuitizing or "W" if you plan on making withdrawals. The purchase of a rider usually confer withdrawal privileges.
- Death Benefit: Yes or No
- Enhanced Death Benefit: Yes or No
- COLA: % increase or formula to calculating the increase
- LTC Coverage: Yes or No
- Carrier Ranking: Use a score from a rating service (note which rating service and try to use the same rating service for each annuity). Not all rating services rate all carriers so there may be some research needed here.

All of these items are from Section B, Step 3: Fine Tune Additional Considerations. Review as necessary. Make sure you are always comparing apples to apples. For example, if you are planning on purchasing an annuity with a COLA feature, make sure all the

Guaranteed Payout Amounts reflect the initial COLA payout. The Guaranteed Payout Amount with a COLA feature will start lower than a level payout without a COLA adjustment.

Put the information for each annuity product in a separate column. When happy with the amount of quotes you have collected, rank the features according to your priorities (1 is the highest priority, 10 is the lowest):

- High Guaranteed Payout Amount
- Low Fees
- Low Surrender Charge Period
- Annuitization method of Distribution
- Withdrawal method of Distribution
- A Death Benefit
- An Enhanced Death Benefit
- A COLA adjustment feature
- LTC Coverage feature
- High Carrier Rating

If a feature is not at all important to you, rank it 0. You can have multiple features ranked 0. Make sure the annuities you are considering have the features you rank. For instance, if you are looking at SPIAs, do not rank Withdrawal Method of Distribution as desirable, as SPIAs only use the Annuitization method. Some of the features are only available with the purchase of an additional rider. If you are not willing to purchase the rider, the feature will not be available to you.

Once you have decided what your priorities are, you can search your worksheet for the annuity best fitting your preferential profile. For instance, if you decide a high payout is of primary importance to you, search for the annuity with the highest payout and highlight it. Do the same for your other priorities, marking the best in each category. Ignore those category that are unimportant to you. After completion, you should be able to see which annuity has the highest number of "best of" in relation to your priorities. After seeing the results you will be able to make a clear, informed decision as to which product would be best for you.

APPENDIX B

NOTES FOR OBTAINING QUOTES FROM DIFFERENT SOURCES

Your success in using the process outlined in this book will mostly hinge on your ability to obtain not only good information but the same type of information about each product.

As an annuity is an insurance product, quotes from an annuity sales adviser will be provided to you via something called an illustration. An illustration can be anywhere from 1-20+ pages of information (although the trend is toward fewer pages, not more) detailing a description of the product and what can be currently expected as far as the performance of the product.

The illustration is non-binding and is subject to change at any time before purchase of the product. So if you are collecting quotes and you let more than a couple of weeks pass between obtaining quotes, the earlier illustrations you received may already be out of date.[29]

Also, because the illustration is non-binding, if you use the information on it to select a certain product, it is of utmost importance that you immediately compare the terms on the illustration to the terms on the actual annuity contract you receive after purchase. If there is a discrepancy, you want to know about it during the "free look" period so you can void the contract if the terms are different and are no longer acceptable to you. Ideally, your annuity sales adviser would alert you to any changes in the illustration before you purchase (if it has been more than a few weeks since the illustration was sent to you) and ideally your annuity sales adviser would carefully check over the actual contract for discrepancies but it can't hurt to have a second look at it.

The most important thing to remember is that the quotes must be comparing the same features. There's no sense comparing an annuity funded with $100K to an annuity funded with $150K. Or comparing a Guaranteed Payout figure @ year 10 with a

---

29 In other words, the terms of the annuity may have already changed. This may be especially true if the first quotes you received were obtained shortly before the end of the month; many carriers change specifications (if they are to be changed at all) at the beginning of the month.

Guaranteed Payout figure @ year 5. Just doesn't make sense. You must be consistent with the information you gather.

To help maintain the consistency of your information, use the worksheet from my website: www.AlessandraDerniat.com. You can use it when speaking to annuity sales advisers over the phone, or on your own when searching the Internet for suitable products. A local adviser will probably want a face-to-face meeting and will bring illustrations to leave with you. If you are obtaining a quote over the phone, see if the adviser will email you an illustration after the conversation. All the information you need to fill out the worksheet should be on the illustration.

INDEX

A

B

C

D

F

G

J

L

W

ABOUT THE AUTHOR

Alessandra "Sandy" Derniat is a passionate and often outspoken advocate for consumers in the financial services arena.

A former educator and life-long serial entrepreneur, she currently is a Certified Annuity Specialist, a multi-state licensed life insurance professional, and the Managing Director of Austin-Ross Investment Advisory LLC (a California Registered Investment Adviser firm).

Sandy resides in the San Diego, California metropolitan area.

CONTACT SANDY

Questions or constructive comments about the content of this book? Email BookTalk@AlessandraDerniat.com

Would you like information about Sandy's educational webinar based on this book? Email TeachMe@AlessandraDerniat.com

Interested in having Sandy speak to your group? Email TalkToUs@AlessandraDerniat.com

To set a mutually convenient time to speak personally with Sandy email TalkToSandy@AlessandraDerniat.com

For the companion worksheet for this book and to learn more about Sandy and her work, please visit
www.AlessandraDerniat.com

47461495R00069

Made in the USA
Lexington, KY
06 December 2015